lotus

the lotus is not just the flower.

it's the whole bush with its leaves and stems in the water
and its roots underneath the mud. it's the sun from the
sky, it's the air and the soil around. it's the seed it once
was and the seeds it's going to become.
this colorful and fragrant beauty of a blossom includes
everything that made it the way it is.

we have learned to only cherish the flower and deemed
the unseen nourishment and the underworld of roots as
negative, to the extent that we even fail to see them as
nourishment and roots in the first place.
but the bush only grows as far above as it grows deep
below, all in its own unique timing.

may this book be a reminder that all that we are –
resistant, annoyed, hopeless, fearful, crying, screaming,
shaking, puking, tired, soft, intuitive, brave, clear,
heartful, caring, vibrant, celebrating – is not only
worthy of our love, but an essential ingredient for our
human nature to fully blossom.

Kristi Pokorny

lotus

BIRTHED THROUGH MUD

Bibliographic information of the German National Library:
The German National Library lists these publications in the
German National Bibliography; Detailed bibliographic data are
available on the internet via http: //dnb.dnb.de.

Production: BoD · Books on Demand GmbH, In de Tarpen 42,
22848 Norderstedt
Print: Libri Plureos GmbH, Friedensallee 273, 22763 Hamburg
ISBN: 978-3-7693-0451-0

to all the brave souls
who dare to wander
through this plane of existence
with a wild and open heart

my heart was broken
by lovers
friends
family
history
society
and i collected
the shattered pieces
only to realize
that it was not
my heart that broke
it was the walls
around it

contents

here i am
hurt
lonely
lost
and i bathe in it

MUD

she was wandering
through the skies
spotting the umber
in his eyes
blurred by waves
building an
unreachable surface

down the water
she reached her wings
while he was jumping
into the sky's beginnings

they touched
and felt
the other realm's
heart beating
being remembered
of the love
they will never
truly be meeting

...

...

perceiving his beauty
and the mystery
of his core
sensing the gravity
of her internal war

she left him a spark
of the star-filled heights
he left her the glory
of the depth and the wise

peeling off
the last bits of her
shattered hope
she flew off
to the places
where she truly
belonged

was it really just hormones
or was it two souls
whose humanness
couldn't hold the paradise
they were tasting?

waking up next to him
felt like infinite vacation
she didn't deserve

she took a big leap
into his muddy pond
of confusion
and drowned

she forced harmony
not to feel her pain

he forced disharmony
not to feel his

sometimes hopes match
but realities don't

she was able to see
his raw and innocent heart
underneath the thick layer of scars
that blinded his sight
and turned their divine dance
into an infinite fight

with him
she was somewhere between
fuck yes
fuck you
and
what the fuck

she couldn't spit it
into his face
but at least
she can spit it
onto paper

he demonized her storm
while its only purpose was
to destroy everything
that prevented his flowers
from growing

he loved her drama
because it made him feel alive

he hated her drama
because it made him feel alive

oh how she would love
to be the bridge
that makes his tears
cross from eye
over the stormy seas
of shame and fear
back to mother earth

she stopped
fighting their battles
and crying their waterfalls
and soon
their scars
made her the enemy

he tried to make her smile
as if his life depended on it

but

all she needed was to cry
as if her life depended on it

when she was happy
he was happy

when she was sad
he was gone

love means
understanding
and compassion

until both
break you

and love means
to just leave

he pretended
he was pure gold

but as soon as
the shimmering elixir
of her melting eyes
kissed the surface
of his shiny polish
it slowly vanished
and dissolved
into an auburn landscape
of flaky rust

he was a natural disaster
with the eyes
of a shaman

a dangerous battlefield
with the voice
of a preacher man

a devilish force
with the hands
of a healer

and she molded herself
for his
eyes
voice
hands

she turned into a mask
to please his mask

and didn't give herself
the chance
to experience the opposite
of catastrophe

stop playing the victim
said the villain

she was willing
to break
her legs
arms
and every single fucking bone
for him

but he was aiming for her heart

if medusa were a man
he'd be it

he was fine
with her being aphrodite
as long as
she kept herself hidden
in the shadow of patriarchy

the fear
he never wanted to admit:

*you can be a woman
just not too loud*

how dare you
explain an ocean
what a drop is

she
blossoming
when he is not around
means
he is not the right soil

he tasted like
the juicy colors
of a flower meadow
touched by the warm rays
of the summer sun
flooded with the crisp air
from the gentle breeze
of god's loving breath
and yet
he was poison

she thought
he was salve
but he was salt

he asked her
to cover up her body
only to conceal
his own lack
of self-esteem

he kept reminding her
of how weak she is
and never considered
she may need the opposite
to grow strong

he stabbed her
right into the heart
only to fall to the ground
and blame her for bleeding

stop making your mirror hers

do you really want a man
that rather sees your mask
than your face?

he carried a lot of shame
and thought
loading it onto her
will free him

don't mold her
hold her

if you don't love my roots
you love nothing

how can i forgive someone

who enters my holy temple
with the smell
of carrion and cigars
covering up
the soft lavender scent
from my freshly lit incense?

who steps
with his muddy and stinky feet
onto the carefully laid-out
red silk carpet

and knocks over
the beautifully decorated
porcelain vases filled with
pink lilies and white roses?

someone who spits
onto my buffet
of lovingly prepared delicacies

...

...

who destroys
the hand-made golden chandelier
hanging from the stucco ceiling
and turns the warm light
into a black hole?

someone who disrupts
the peacefully chanted lullabies
by choking
on my most precious instrument
and summons
the cries of the past instead?

ultimately someone
who enters my sacred space
and ruthlessly leaves it in ashes?

tell me god

how can i forgive someone
like that?

and even more so

how can i forgive myself
for letting him in
in the first place?

do you really worry about her?
or are you just afraid
that she might be right?

they say she is crazy
what they mean is
we are afraid

maybe they're right

maybe she is
a ticking time bomb

and maybe it's her time
to finally explode
and let them
swallow her fire

so many men
trying to save her
when all she needs
is love

fuel her
don't fool her

there is always a reason
behind her anger

the biggest is
you doubting it

you blaming her anger
is you burning her witches

i am sorry
for every time
i declared myself
as crazy
when in fact
i was simply right

she doesn't carry
the pain of one woman
in the here and now

she carries the pain
of all women
in the
there and now
here and then
there and then

remember that

she walks
with her bleeding heart
in her bare hands
and still walks

she went through hell
to gain trust
from its residents

her cells are libraries
that carry
novels upon novels
about how one
can hate themselves

she might spend
her entire life
on replacing
those books
with love letters

it's normal
that you feel shame
for your truth
when all it did
in the past
was to put you
in danger

use your trauma
as explanation
not as an excuse

her wounds were tired
of dancing the tango
with other wounds

danger does not become peace
just because it gets familiar

rushing into peace
is just another expression
of war

when danger was your normal
everything despite that
seems suspicious

the devil is a starving child

what better muse is there
than hell?

art is a necessity
in a world
falling apart

depreciating your art
is
abandoning your children

her fear was wrapped
in shiny gift paper
of overflowing kindness

she desperately
wanted them
to see her
but forgot
that she has eyes
too

this world needs male tears

every inch
he is moving away
from his pain
is a destruction
to the world

oh how she grieves
for every tear
that hasn't left the eye
due to shame and fear

will you be with me
in times
when not even
i
can be with myself?

you can see her
as your biggest mistake
or your greatest learning
- your choice

he was a catalyst
for her dreams
and a knife
to her wounds

now she decides
which she keeps
and which she drops

she did
what made systems
collapse
behind her

she paused

THROUGH

alone
in the dark

breathing out
the echoes of the old
scratching off
the last pieces of useless crust
letting go of the weight
of not listening inward
not tuning in
not holding space

and slowly
gently
gracefully
getting ready for a new adventure

an adventure
that no one can witness
except for her
strong, lovely, innocent and pure
heart

it all starts here and now
with her
sitting on the windowsill

alone

play and cry
this is her new chapter

bye

and the drops
on her window pane said:

stop fighting your tears
little girl

don't you see

god cries too

no rainbows without rain
no magic without tears

tears are
frozen hearts
melting

when she feels for herself
she feels for everyone

rock bottom was waiting for her

but not in the way
she imagined it would

not in a
"i am going to appear like a bloody
man-eating monster, ripping your flesh apart,
breaking your bones, smashing your face in
and then throwing you into a big pile of crap"
- kind of way

no

more like a dear lover

with rose petals on the cold stone
and candles by the old wooden doorway
cozy blankets in the gloomy corners
and heart-soothing water
in the sharp cracks

...

...

rock bottom is like
the middle of a tornado

everything around you
is falling apart

but you

you stand still
time stands still

rock bottom wraps you in his
warm, loving and strong arms
makes your heart soften
and lets your head release
all the doubt
that it was anything
but pure love

her demons know
so much better than she does
the way through
the enchanted labyrinth
towards heaven

fighting your trauma
is cutting off your roots

it's not about him
not deserving your anger
or grief
or despair

it's about all that
wanting to finally deserve you

your love
your presence
your patience

let him go
and be the kind of lover
he never wanted to be for you

voltaire said
he has chosen to be happy
because it is good for his health

and i wonder how?

how can i choose a smile
when my body in fact
wants to shrink into the size
of a moth's cocoon
and refuses to make any contact
with daylight?

voltaire puts it so effortlessly

as if happiness is a leaf
you can simply pick
from a common tree

but to me

it feels like a long forgotten language
whose words
i needed to scratch off
of gray, wet pavement
and broken window panes

...

...

to form phrases
that maybe lasted
for a blink of an eye
when i was lucky

the texture
the taste
the smell

i had to learn that

and yes
in some moments it's easy
to drop a sentence and hold a speech

but then there are times
when my lips
simply forget how to speak

how can i choose something
that so easily
slips through my fingers?

yes, i could try to remember
but why would i run after something
that never lingers?

...

...

instead i can decide
to fall in love
with all the other words
that fall from above

with my pain, my grief
my boredom, my anger
with the aching in my head
the tensing in my chest
the salt on my face
the shaking in my legs

all that slips through too, anyways

in the end
there is no language
that ever stays

so instead of fixating on something
that never lasts
i'd rather learn to sing songs
in different tongues

it may not be healthy
and it may sound odd

but at least
it makes me melt with god

even if the world ran out of water
i'd still have my tears

people do not need solutions
they need permission

there is anger
that turns into walls

anger
that turns into tears

and then there is anger
that solely exists
as pure expression

she didn't have
any other choice
than to sit
and listen
and let all the monsters
have their show
as long as they needed to

honey,

i'm not the one who tells you
that you don't need to feel ashamed
or gifts you a list
of twenty reasons
why you are a worthy being

i am the one who throws you
right into the pure, icy water
of deep surrender

i let you drown in it
and let your body crumble

until you realize
that the feeling of shame
was never the enemy

nor was your resistance to it

...

...

my dear
there is no enemy
no need to fight

so no

i'm not the one who tells you
you don't need to feel ashamed

i am the one who tells you

you need it
more than anything else

and it needs you
more than anything else

merge

- sincerely, love

she was pulled into
the depths and the dark
of the night
as if the moon
needed more
ambassadors of the sun
to shine bright

sometimes
she is jealous
of the dark
because
the way it can
receive light
is supreme

she is everything
in that moment
because
she is with
everything
in that moment

if you think
she needs a pill
baby
it's you
that has never tasted
the sweetness
of full surrender

she doesn't trust the ones
who do not know
how to dance
with their demons

have grace
with everything in you
that believes
that suffering
is safety

cloudy skies
and god loves her

every single hell
is an invitation
to breathe
sink
and fall
deeper
into the pillow
of trust

no trust is born
in the garden of eden
the deepest is born
in the uttermost desert

winter is a flower
that blossoms too

if you let her

the picture in her windowpane
was sunrays upon a summer field
with juicy fruits as color splashes

while
she was all about
gray and cozy winter mood
filled with waterfalls from her eyes

drops got deeply buried
under white soil
where her little calm and quiet
cocoon of a seed was nourished
without the need to spoil
god's magic
happening effortlessly, naturally

no growth perceived
no wonder witnessed

just trust
that one day
she'll wake up
and her window will watch her
celebrate spring
no matter the picture
on the outside

their nothing
is her rendezvous
with god

she let the rays
of the nearby sun
and the warmth
of the summer night's breeze
hold space
for her
deep and lonely
internal winter
to flourish

self-care is revolution

god forced her
into deep and dark
loneliness
only to befriend her

she stopped drowning
the moment
she let herself drown

you cannot dance it away
but you can dance it

her blood
and her tears
are her
artistic
elixirs

while they go
bigger
faster
higher
she goes
slow
v e r y s l o w

she is busy
not being busy

the desert turned into an oasis
when she turned into the now

feel to feel
not to heal

hearts are not sticks
they are pillows
you can't break them

she is going
through an expression

it's like a depression

just a little bit more
loud, wild and free

she cries
on the streets
the bus
the dance floor

she does not hide
her humanness
just because the world
is afraid of its own

she found the holy grail —
 a dance
 between
 a breath
 and
 a body

how raw can you go?

stop following advice
from people
who don't embody
the physical
mental
emotional
financial
or spiritual
health
you want to achieve

let their talk bounce off
and silently carry on
with your craziness

she took all their judgments
burned them
warmed her cold feet
and got ready to embark
with softness and resilience
on her soul's path

she's giving up
all people and places
that need translation
for her soul's language

in order to understand the storm
she needed to become it

her rage liberates all women
inside
outside
behind
and ahead
of her

oh, how she used to love
taking on the responsibility
of feeling all the pain
they did not allow themselves
to feel on their own

and how she loves it even more
to simply stop

if anger is her truth
that's what the world needs

you will never be able
to meditate anger away

never

(except for the one that is not yours)

being an asshole
is the easy way

being a pleaser
is the easy way

try to be raw

it will rip
all the masks
within and without you
apart

what if you dont' need approval

from your past
other people
your circumstances
the moon
the star constellations
the season
the weather

to allow yourself
to feel a certain way?

what if
simply feeling
what you feel
is enough reason
to deserve your love?

no thirst without water
no longing without paradise

he didn't see shadows
under her eyes
he saw rainbows

if she only knew
how deeply and thoroughly
god is celebrating her wild
in every single now

the bigger the heart
the heavier the quake
after every beat

her crystal clear
blue eyes
make rivers
floating out of them
look like waterfalls
from the sky

her wings
are hungry
for art

if they won't love me
i will

BIRTHED

their brown eyes
taught her what love is
taught her what love is not
but most of all they taught her
that no matter what
the strength of the soil
shall carry her soul
the motion of the sea
reflects her own
and the lucidity of the air
will always assure

with or without them
you're home

yes
this love made us sick
turned us into
vomiting monsters

but isn't every flu
just a necessary purge
of all the waste
that has been stuck inside
for too long?

can you really say
it's against you
when all it does
is set you free?

she is done
with people
not valuing
her walk
her talk
her presence

and more so

she is done
with herself
not doing so either

when she finally moved
in the rhythm of her needs
all the matches
that only matched
the rhythm of her masks
burned away

your yes
needs
a very
frequent
no

saying no to people
that do not
embrace your flaws
is saying yes
to all of you

choosing to love
doesn't mean
choosing to stay

if you want orange juice
stop settling for apple trees

she'd rather miss him
than herself

she learned
that giving up the ones
that gave up themselves
is not evil

it's necessary

you mastered falling in love
with potentials

now you can master waiting

until you fall for the one
that already embodies them

people that are good for you
do not appear good

they *feel* good

surround yourself
with people
that steadily
remind you
of how precious
you are

if you ain't making my story
more poetic
there is no place for you
in my book

it's in her exhale
that tells her
how much of a man
he is

actions do not speak
louder than words

energy does

if it's not a clear
and all-mighty
yes

it's a no
or a not yet

trust that

she is ready
for the kind
of adventure
that is her own

she will never be able
to break a heart
by following hers

for that may only
break rules

she wants to wake up
every single morning
with the feeling of purpose

until she doesn't have that
she won't stop moving

she doesn't know
what she is searching for
but she knows
that she wants to search

she'd rather seek
all her life
for something
unknown and uncertain
than to settle
for very definite shit
right away

she doesn't settle
because she knows
that she will know
when it's time to

she won't settle
for anything less
than her tribe

she already
has a feeling
to a feeling
she has never felt

[home]

now i am just waiting

until not only every inch
of my heart
feels a yes

but also every bit
of my heart's
shattered pieces

more and more
parts of her
choose the dance
with the mystery

leaving her
wondrous
and curious
a little scared
and nervous

but most of all
filled with purpose

she dropped the concepts
and met god

i choose truth
i choose truth
i choose truth

in every single move

i refuse the shoulds
from machine heads

fuck those high extensions
and supposedly evolved bendings

if god wants me to throw my leg
i will

if god wants me to arch my back
i will

if god wants me to only breathe
stick out my tongue
grab my breasts
and my pussy
shake like a maniac
scream like a hyena
i will do so

and the voices that resist
my dance with the divine
are free to dance their dance
or to utterly join

she used to be the one
that conformed to everything

now she seems to be the one
that breaks it all

she attracted the ones
that were ready for her chaos
when she began
celebrating it herself

her head will never be able
to define the places
birthed by heart

and she remembered
that her dreams
need as much attention
as her wounds

your pain deserves you
so does your bliss

she rises
because
she sank
deeper

she starts believing
that she's here to experience

reality that feels like vacation
work that feels like satiation
family gatherings that feel like celebration
nature walks that feel like salvation
relationships that feel like elevation
passions that feel like liberation

a life full of dedication
to the beauty of all creation

are you ready? - god asks

choose
the parallel reality
that feeds your soul

she won't go back
to the place
where self-care
isn't a priority

yin and yang
baby
yin and yang

allow yourself to be soft
and i promise you
i will turn into
a marvelous
juicy
powerful
pleasure bomb

- your yoni

she stopped running
and finally
her dreams
could catch her

one day she heard
her privilege whispering:

use me baby

the waiting room
is her art lab

take care of your art
and your art
will take care of you

if your art
is not for yourself
it's for no one

art
  - the collision
  between the finish
  and the start

be the kind of embarrassing
that makes sense to you

preach that
which you can sign
with your blood

and one day
she decided
that the world
needs her

going nowhere slow

i am not going to wait
for the best version of me
to occur
to begin loving myself

i'll start now

this between you and me
is not over yet

we may not talk anymore

you may not caress my skin
in the morning
while my ear is pressed
against your chest

you may not stand in the kitchen
gifting me with your
culinary magnificence

we may not let time
stand still together
and turn a nature trip
into heaven on earth

that all may be over now

yes

but you and me?

us?

...

...

we will never be gone

us lives in every single breath i take
in every emotion i release
in every brave decision i make
in every little art piece i create

i feel your presence
see you applauding
hear your judgement
smell your fear

with every single step
i am moving towards myself
your hand is holding mine

and i won't let go

because even though
you ripped me apart
in the most painful way
you also catapulted me
right into my heart
in the most needed one

...

...

so no

you and me are not over yet

and i believe we never will be

because there will always be
a place in my heart
with a bright campfire for us
celebrating the life we shared
the paradise we tasted together

the you within me
that made me more of myself

thank you for your bright light
making my mind blind
so all i could rely on
was my humble, mysterious,
magical and wild

heart sight

she is an infinite erupting volcano
with truth as her lava
a bunch of ever-growing wildflowers
with trust as her blossoms
a kinder egg of endless surprises
with pleasure as her toy
god's intention has never been
to tame her
his intention always has been
and always will be
to love her

LOTUS

there are days i wake up
and feel perfectly fine

i look forward to my breakfast
to greeting the ones i love
and to my life

i see everything that is beautiful
within me and around
excited to get up
and make this day count

and then i hesitate

because i remember this girl
a few years ago
she did not believe in a world
where one wakes up and feels alive
dances with sun rays
and dares to thrive

all she experienced
was her body being tight
staying up all night
with her thoughts in a constant fight

hating herself and thus the day
closing off and shutting down
wishing to simply decay

...

...

but at least she could pray

for something unknown
something she's never been shown
some distant echo in her ear

she wondered
whether she shall keep going
or fall for her fear
that the light at the end of the tunnel
may just be a candle
ready to burn down
something she may not be able to handle
that would finally make her drown

but she kept surviving tear after tear
and now she is here

now she is here

infiltrating my cells
with warm honey and glitter

with the voice of an angel
i hear us whisper

thank you

her chaos is healing the world

sunrise and solar eclipse
tides and landslide
hurricane and earthquake

this is just a glimpse
of the tremendous miracle nature is

nature is way too wild
to be held together
with screws, nails and rubber-band

nature selfishly, unpredictably
expresses itself
and doesn't care about
any statistics or forecasts

so does life
so does her animal body
and so does her feral soul

they erupt, flow, grow, steam, shrink,
crunch, dance, sigh, shake, harden,
soften, widen, contract, release ...

maybe she was never supposed
to change that

maybe she was only meant
to turn that into art

she doesn't create art
her soul just pukes

she does not know about
names and dates

all she remembers
is essence and taste

who taught you that?

life
life taught me that

her body is like science
just a little more trustworthy

flashing arteries from the sky
and god is a man-made concept?

there is nothing
more mundane
than magic

she loves three things

honesty
honesty
honesty

real vibes
over good vibes

seventy percent
of our body
is made of water

of course
her eyes are geysers
her breath is waves
and her life
is a mixture
of melting ice blocks
stormy currents
and dense forest mist

remember that you are the goddess

he caresses
her round landscapes
and sharp crevasses
like an archaeologist
embarking on a
divine exploration
through the garden of eden
and the universe
between her legs
remembers paradise

i am devoted
to fall in love with myself
deeper and deeper

so i will be able
to receive the love
you carry for me

i know your love
is not a little oil lamp

your love is
moonbeam and sunrise
fireflies and starry skies
embers and polar lights

i let myself be opened up
and emptied by life

so i become
a vessel of god's love

so i become
a holy receiver of yours

there is a storm
roaming around our heart

a storm of stories and lies

of old waste covering up
all the magic and mystery
we are meant to experience

this life has never been
a life of control
and perfectly measured outcomes

it has always been a miraculous ride
through glitter and mud

the storm has so many answers
to the questions that it created itself

...

...

but it has never had
and will never have
the wisdom
of the heart it surrounds

for only the heart
knows what she knows
and brings you back
to the places you truly seek to be

wonder, bliss, grace, beauty, joy,
fun, abundance, fulfillment, truth,
connection, ease, peace, love, home

only heart
will guide you home

and only heart knows
that you already are

sometimes her heart
speaks in phrases
that feel like fog
to her cognitive places

she lets those walls
around her heart
gradually fall

she knows
it needs its air
to grow
the fire
that lights up
everything
that is used to walls

every single body part of hers
is fragile like achilles' heel

except for her little heart

that one is stronger
than any steel

she is married to her heart
because not even death
will do them apart

what if there is no clear why?

what if the why
is your heart yelling at you
that if you do not do
that one thing
that it is aching for
it simply feels like betrayal?

what if there is no goal
no future destination
you are heading towards
but simply the deep desire
of wandering
through the waves of life
with your open heart
as your safest guide
blindfolded but fully trusting?

...

...

what if you don't know
what you want to achieve
in ten years
but if you know
that your destination
is an ever molding surprise
that changes its color and form
with every single step in the now?

what if your dreams
promise you nothing more
than what you currently have
except for being more
of who you currently are?

and what if all that
is not only enough
but everything?

her favorite season is the now

sitting on the september meadow
the sunset lake in her eyes

- *she is home*

her favorite movie is nature

there is much more magic
in the gaze of a deer
than there will ever be
in skyscrapers
fashion
or beer

she finally
entered a realm
where she realizes
that not movement
makes her a dancer

life does

a million pills in the pharmacy
and she chooses dance

dance is the natural phenomenon
of letting life force fully in

what kind of dance do you dance?

- god. i dance god

do you move to look good
or do you move to feel good?

- *both*

she doesn't turn
into a wild beast
when she is dancing

she just turns
into a machine
when she is not

she'd rather be
a natural disaster
than a machine

she has the capacity
to contain
the depth
of wilderness
that was stoned
burned
and haunted
for being embodied

her deepest roots
are made of their soil

their beating hearts
innocent and pure

soft and fragile

oceans of forgotten tears

she loves them
she loves them
she loves them

[lineage]

burning witches
is like
burning the sun

deep down she knows
that her fire
is not supposed
to light a candle

her fire is supposed
to make systems collapse

she is the dance
between
the collapse
and the birth
of a universe

she always wants more

let her

she feels like depth
because she is

of course they perceive her
as crazy

she is here to change
the paradigm

she is a drama queen
so what

i burnt most of my art

some on the pyre of
not even worth it to create

others in the dry woods of
not good enough

a bunch in the red-hot oven of
lack of bravery

and the last
i simply offered to god

so what you see, hear and feel
is a drop
a teeny tiny little bit
of a drop
of the ocean that has flooded
through my brush, my pencil,
my breath and my veins already

...

...

these masterpieces
were not created
for anything or anyone
but my cells

i am an artist

they know that
the fire knows
and god

and when i'm ready

i'll let the world know
too

her secret is
this isn't just a phase

it's her life

healing is not her purpose

living is

we deserve the kind of love
that feels like
a light summer breeze
gently kissing every single inch
of our vivid skin

the kind of love
where the wildest raging storms
are calling us back home
and rooting our hearts even deeper
into the soil of trust and faith

where the highest truths
come with the greatest safety
where the strongest bond
comes with the
sincerest form of freedom

a love that does not
leave us speechless
but gives us the power
to scream louder

...

...

a love where the gifts
do not come from giving
but from being

a love that celebrates
the purest form
of our existence

that leads us out of the labyrinth
of sorrow and worry
and slowly pulls us onto the path
of magic and mystery

we deserve the kind of love
without question marks

the kind of love that embraces
every cell of our body
with the warmth and softness
of a subtle and yet fierce

yes

to me
there is no life before poetry

there is only life after

she made it through
once
twice
a million times

her flowers bloom
all over again

with every birth
new colors and fragrances
are painted and anointed
on her body

her roots grow deeper
her leaves grow bigger
and more space is created
to make love
to earth
to sun
and the magic around

at her highest
she kisses her deepest
takes both by her hand
smiles and remembers

this is her life

the end

dear reader
my soul feels honored being held
in your presence throughout the lines
of this book
from my heart to your heart:
gratitude

Acknowledgments

Thank you to my beautiful sister Sindi for your great artistic sense, for letting yourself be touched by my words, for supporting me with the cover choice, for simply being proud of me, and for being you.

Thank you to my dear friends Jana and Josh for lending me your English expertise and assisting with the refinement of my poems. Asking for help is not easy for me, and I am grateful to feel safe doing it with you.

Another deep thanks goes to my parents for supporting me in every way they can, even though they have no clue what the hell I am doing. Ju dua shumë.

Thank you, Lena, for continuously reminding me to let go of control and lean back into the hands of God. This book would not have been created without you.

And Eva — your boundless compassion and our podcast have been a healing companion, inspiration and support during the times of unraveling myself in the midst of shattering and opening. I am deeply grateful for you and us.

I also thank life itself for gifting me with all the people and experiences that broke and healed me, for giving me the chance and the space to grow into a more truthful, trusting, and loving version of myself.
You truly drive me wild, but well, you know …
wild is just my taste.

hello@kristipokorny.com

@kristipoetry